The use of too many  avoided, as it is more encourage comment to expect particular answers.

Care has been taken to retain sufficient realism in the illustrations and subject matter to enable a young child to have fun identifying objects, creatures and situations.

It is wise to remember that patience and understanding are very important, and that children do not all develop evenly or at the same rate. Parents should not be anxious if children do not give correct answers to those questions that are asked. With help, they will do so in their own time.

 The brief notes at the back of this book will enable interested parents to make the fullest use of these **Ladybird talkabout** books.

Ladybird Books Ltd   Loughborough 1976

Richard

compiled by Margaret West

illustrated by Harry Wingfield

The publishers wish to acknowledge the assistance of
the nursery school advisers who helped with the
preparation of this book,
especially that of Mrs Nora Britton, Chairman,
and Miss M Puddephat, M Ed, Vice Chairman
of The British Association for Early Childhood
Education (formerly The Nursery School Association).

talkabout
gardens

Talk about the garden

Playing in the garden

The garden in spring

Birds in the garden

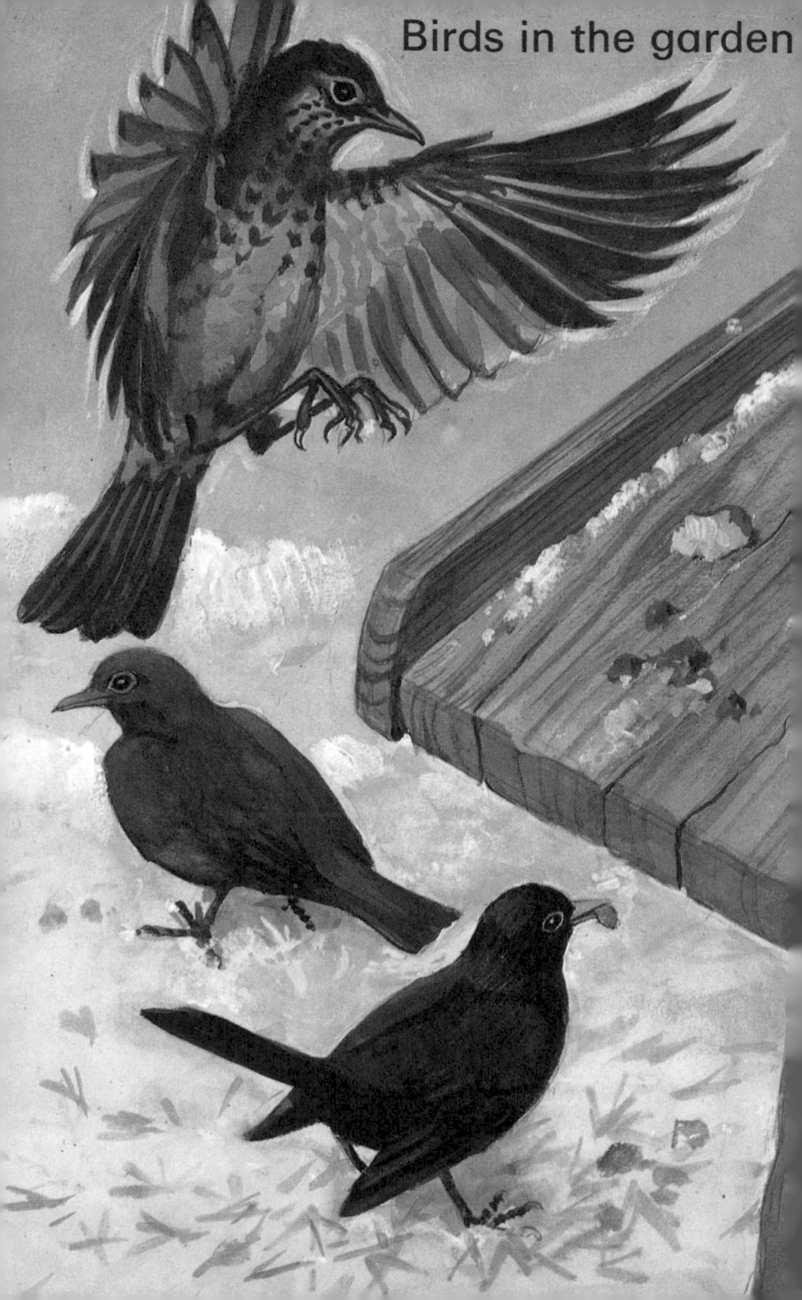

Match each picture with its black shape

Talk about insects
in the garden

LOOK and find
another
like this

. . . and this

. . . and this

Growing radishes

LOOK and find
another like this

. . . and this

. . . and this

Talk about potatoes

1

2

Talk about
flowers
from bulbs

Put the bulbs in damp fibre
and store in a dark, **cool** place

Now they are ready to come out and flower

Tell the story

Have y

ted these ?

Talk abo

tall a

lar

one a

ort
d small
uny

Watching things grow

Have you smelt these?

Gardens in the park

Talk about what we grow in the greenhouse

Let's make a garden

with an old tray, a small mirror,
stones, twigs, grass or moss, soil
and a few small flowers

The garden shop

seeds

Suggestions for extending the use of this **talkabout** book . . .

There are many ways in which the illustrations in this book may be used — the page headings are intended only as brief suggestions.

Each picture has been planned not only to extend the child's vocabulary but also his understanding of concepts. In this book you can talk about the value of water, the usefulness of insects, comparative sizes, taste, and how things grow. You can also talk about time, balance, tidiness and numbers, leading into each subject with a particular picture, and illustrating it further from other pictures.

Visual differences of shape may be pointed out from many of the illustrations, such as 'Look and find another like this' and 'Match